A Note to Parents

DK READERS is a compelling program for beginning readers, designed in conjunction with leading literacy experts, including Dr. Linda Gambrell, Distinguished Professor of Education at Clemson University. Dr. Gambrell has served as President of the National Reading Conference, the College Reading Association, and the International Reading Association.

Beautiful illustrations and superb full-color photographs combine with engaging, easy-to-read stories to offer a fresh approach to each subject in the series. Each DK READER is guaranteed to capture a child's interest while developing his or her reading skills, general knowledge, and love of reading.

The five levels of DK READERS are aimed at different reading abilities, enabling you to choose the books that are exactly right for your child:

Pre-level 1: Learning to read
Level 1: Beginning to read
Level 2: Beginning to read alone
Level 3: Reading alone
Level 4: Proficient readers

The "normal" age at which a child begins to read can be anywhere from three to eight years old. Adult participation through the lower levels is very helpful for providing encouragement, discussing storylines, and sounding out unfamiliar words.

No matter which level you select, you can be sure that you are helping your child learn to read, then read to learn!

DK

LONDON, NEW YORK, MUNICH,
MELBOURNE, AND DELHI

Senior Editor Helen Murray
Designer Lauren Rosier
Jacket Designer Lauren Rosier
Design Manager Ron Stobbart
Publishing Manager Catherine Saunders
Art Director Lisa Lanzarini
Publisher Simon Beecroft
Publishing Director Alex Allan
Production Editor Andy Hilliard
Production Controller Melanie Mikellides
Reading Consultant Dr. Linda Gambrell

First published in the United States in 2012
by DK Publishing
375 Hudson Street
New York, New York 10014
10 9 8 7 6 5 4 3 2 1
LEGO and the LEGO logo are trademarks of the LEGO Group.
© 2012 the LEGO Group.
Produced by Dorling Kindersley
under license from the LEGO Group.

001—184097—July/12

DK books are available at special discounts when purchased
in bulk for sales promotions, premiums, fund-raising, or
educational use.
For details, contact:
DK Publishing Special Markets
375 Hudson Street
New York, New York 10014
SpecialSales@dk.com

A catalog record for this book is available
from the Library of Congress.

ISBN: 978-0-7566-9382-4 (Paperback)
ISBN: 978-0-7566-9383-1 (Hardcover)

Color reproduction by Media Development and Printing, UK
Printed and bound in the USA by Lake Book Manufacturing, Inc.

Discover more at
www.dk.com
www.LEGO.com

Contents

DK READERS

Friends Forever

Written by Helen Murray

A new home

Heartlake City is a wonderful place to live. Whether you love nature, relaxation, shopping, or going to cool parties and events, you are sure to find lots to do in this beautiful city. For one lucky girl, Heartlake City has just become her new home. Her name is Olivia and she is looking forward to all the fun and excitement the city promises.

Olivia can't wait to plan an outdoor adventure in the mountains, take a boat out onto Lake Heart, and go to open-air concerts in the park. But, most of all, Olivia is excited to make lots of new friends. With all the cool things to do in her new city, that should be no problem at all!

There are many different types of beautiful buildings in Heartlake City.

Rocket

Olivia

Olivia has just moved to Heartlake City with her parents and their white cat, Missy. Olivia is a clever, hardworking student and she is looking forward to studying at Heartlake School. Her favorite subjects are science, art, and history. Olivia is a practical person who loves to solve problems.

Olivia is always prepared. She carries a few useful tools in her pretty bag!

Missy

Olivia's cat, Missy, is very mischievous. She likes her new home because there are lots of good hiding places to discover!

She likes to make and fix things. One day she hopes to be a scientist, inventor, or engineer.

Olivia enjoys nature and hiking and she is eager to explore the beautiful woods, coastline, and mountains of Heartlake City. Unfortunately, this will have to wait because Olivia's parents have told her that she must unpack all of the boxes in her room first!

Olivia's family moved to Heartlake City because her dad, Peter, got a job as editor of the Heartlake Times. Olivia's mom, Anna, is a doctor.

She also has a new job, at Heartlake City hospital. Anna is a very kind and caring doctor.

Although Olivia's parents both work very hard, they always make time for their daughter. They go for family walks and bike rides, watch movies together, and sometimes help Olivia with her homework—although clever Olivia rarely needs any help!

Olivia's dad is a good listener. Olivia enjoys chatting to him while he tends to his vegetable garden in their new front yard.

A quiet place
Olivia loves her new swing. It has become her favorite place to think or write in her diary.

Olivia lives at Number 30, Heartlake Heights. It is a beautiful, big house with many rooms, including a large kitchen, a cozy family room, and Olivia's bedroom. The house has a huge front yard with a white picket fence, a vegetable garden, and pretty flowers. Olivia's favorite flowers are the pink ones that grow below her bedroom window because they attract beautiful butterflies.

Swing

Grill

There is also a rooftop terrace for sunbathing. Olivia's mom has put up an umbrella—just in case it gets too hot! Olivia's dad likes to cook outside. He has set up the big grill in the yard.

Rooftop terrace

Vegetable garden

Mailbox

Lawn mower

Olivia enjoys discovering new things. She has inherited her mom's love of science and even has her own workshop where she goes to invent.

The workshop has everything a budding scientist and inventor needs to mend, experiment, and create.

Chalkboard

Microscope

Chemist jars

Power tools

Olivia is fascinated by crystals. When she found a crystal on a hike, she could not wait to get home to examine it under her microscope.

There is a work bench with power tools, a vice, and a microscope. Olivia writes ideas and plans for her new creations on the large chalkboard. Olivia has built her very own remote-controlled pet robot called Zobo. She uses a screwdriver to put the finishing touches to him. Next she will oil his joints to make sure he moves smoothly. One day, Olivia hopes to program Zobo to do boring household chores, so she doesn't have to!

Vice

New friends

It has been two months since Olivia moved to Heartlake City. She loves her new town. There is always something fun and exciting happening here! But by far the best thing about her new home is her four fabulous friends.

Olivia   Emma   Stephanie   Andrea

It didn't take Olivia long to meet four of the coolest, smartest, and nicest girls in town—Andrea, Mia, Emma, and Stephanie. The five girls are now the best of friends.

The girls have even formed a Friends Club. They use their many skills and talents to solve all sorts of problems that arise in the city. Whether they are helping to find a runaway horse, fixing a collapsed stage, or planning a cool event in Heartlake City, the girls always have fun. Do you want to meet Olivia's new best friends?

Mia

Andrea

Andrea is the drama queen of the group. She loves to sing, dance, and act, and she often puts on performances for her friends. She dreams of one day becoming a superstar.

Andrea is very musical. Even her clothes have musical notes on them!

Andrea loves to perform on a floodlit stage for all of the city to hear.

Although Andrea is a wonderful dancer and actor, her real passion is music. She sings anywhere and everywhere. She sings on stage, at school, at the café where she works, and sometimes even in the shower!

Andrea will soon be the biggest star in Heartlake City. But Andrea does not plan to stop there—she has set her sights on a world tour.

Even budding superstars can have part-time jobs. Andrea works in the girls' favorite hangout, the City Park Café. She works with Marie, the owner, to make delicious milkshakes, cupcakes, pies, and hamburgers.

Hungry work
Andrea's favorite part of the job is testing the tasty new recipes. This burger and pink cupcake get her approval!

Andrea's tasks also include washing the dishes and sweeping the floor. But even at work, Andrea dreams of stardom. She can often be found singing into the broom handle instead of sweeping or serving customers. Unfortunately for Andrea, the hungry customers are usually more interested in the food than her performance. Andrea's daydreams can also cause her to mix up the orders!

Just across the lake from the City Park Café, Andrea regularly performs at an open-air stage for all of Heartlake City to hear.

Andrea sings in the spotlight under a sign with her name on it—a sign that her talented friend Emma made. But Andrea hopes to one day see her name in lights, on a much bigger stage.

Stereo

Piano

Andrea is a talented composer and piano player as well as a singer. She writes and plays all her own songs.

Andrea is an amazing singer. She always brings the audience to their feet and receives a standing ovation. But nobody cheers as loudly as Emma, Olivia, Stephanie, and Mia!

Spotlight

Microphone

Light

Stage

Emma

Emma is an artist. She loves drawing, fashion, and interior design. She is talented but also very practical. Emma can turn anything she finds into something stylish and beautiful.

Her friends often tell Emma that she is forgetful, but she disagrees. After all, she would never forget to leave the house without accessorizing her outfit!

Emma has a magnificent white horse called Robin. They enter show jumping competitions together across Heartlake City. They practice hard and often win prizes. Of course, even Robin's stable is beautifully furnished—Emma likes to decorate the walls with colorful ribbons.

Emma takes photos of her designs to show her friends. The girls love to see her amazing creations.

Emma's biggest passion is fashion and she has a design studio packed with everything she needs to become the next big fashion designer.

Chest of drawers

Inspiration board

Laptop

Fabric

Lamp

Camera

Tape measure

Design table

Hard at work
Emma uses her laptop to research new ideas and to keep up to date with the latest fashion trends and runway shows.

She works at a large design table where she cuts out materials and sews clothes. She stores fabric, paper, and tools in the large pink and purple chest of drawers. Naturally, everything is color-coordinated in her studio! Emma is always looking for inspiration in Heartlake City. She takes her camera everywhere with her. She puts photos and drawings on the large inspiration board in her studio.

Emma uses her talents to give her friends amazing makeovers. Emma, Andrea, Stephanie, Mia, and Olivia love to go shopping together to find new clothes and accessories and to try out new looks. Their favorite boutique is Butterfly Beauty Shop on Main Street.

Puppy makeover

Emma has found the perfect look for Mia's puppy, Charlie. He is bound to win the Cutest Puppy award at Heartlake City's annual dog show.

The girls shop for barrettes, bows, sunglasses, and other cool accessories. Emma always knows what will look best. Her friends wait for the moment when she says "That's so you!"

Emma sometimes gets a little carried away with giving makeovers. Once she has finished creating new looks for the girls, she likes to give their pets makeovers, too! Luckily, the animals love being pampered.

Mia

Mia is crazy about animals. From mice to horses, and even bugs, Mia loves them all! She works part-time at Heartlake Vet with Olivia's Aunt Sophie. One day, Mia would like to become a vet or an animal trainer.

Mia owns a beautiful pony called Bella and an excitable spotty puppy named Charlie. But she also takes in many stray and injured animals and looks after them in her bedroom.

Mia works hard at Heartlake Vet. She is caring and practical. She would make a great vet!

Mia cares for the animals until they are better or she can find them a loving, new home.

Outdoor girl Mia loves to go camping, canoeing, and horseback riding, of course. She is learning to play the drums too, but she makes sure that there are no animals around when she practices. She doesn't want to scare them or hurt their ears!

Mia's favorite animal is her horse, Bella. She visits Bella in her stable every morning and evening. Mia makes sure that Bella has enough water and food, as well as clean straw to sleep on. Bella needs plenty of exercise, so Mia practices jumping with her, or goes for long rides in the woods. They spend so much time together that Emma sometimes accuses Mia of smelling of horses!

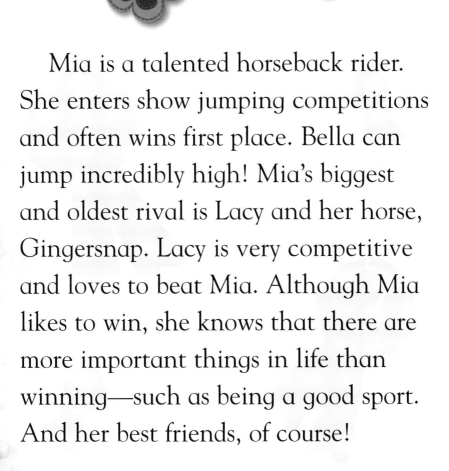

Bella has won countless ribbons and cups for show jumping.

Mia is a talented horseback rider. She enters show jumping competitions and often wins first place. Bella can jump incredibly high! Mia's biggest and oldest rival is Lacy and her horse, Gingersnap. Lacy is very competitive and loves to beat Mia. Although Mia likes to win, she knows that there are more important things in life than winning—such as being a good sport. And her best friends, of course!

Mia has a gift for looking after and training animals. She talks to the animals and they seem to be able to understand her! Animals always bond very quickly with Mia, so this makes training them much easier.

Tasty treat
Mia rewards clever Charlie with a bone for his hard work at the Heartlake City Dog Show.

Mia is training her puppy, Charlie. He is usually very well-behaved, but he does like to run through puddles! He is mostly white, so he gets dirty very quickly. Mia puts him in a tub and cleans him with a brush and special dog shampoo.

Charlie is young and he is still learning new tricks, but he has already mastered the obstacle course at Heartlake City's annual dog show. He has won two awards to prove it!

Stephanie

Stephanie is a born party planner. She loves to organize spectacular events, sleepovers, and adventures with the girls. Stephanie is a great friend to have around—she always gets the girls into the party spirit.

Stephanie can be a little bossy at times, but her friends know that it is just because she wants everything to go perfectly.

However, if anything ever does go wrong, Stephanie takes charge. She knows exactly what to do—and which of her friends should do it!

Stephanie has recently started taking flying lessons at the local flight school. If you see a plane overhead, it might just be her!

Stephanie's dog
Stephanie has a brown puppy called Coco. She makes sure that Coco always looks immaculate!

Stephanie believes that a party is not a party unless there is cake! She is an excellent baker and her cupcakes, birthday cakes, brownies, and pies always look perfect and taste wonderful. Stephanie is far too careful to let anything go wrong.

Cake

Umbrella

Brownie

Milk

Oven

Super-organized Stephanie never forgets her friends' birthdays and always bakes a cake for them.

Stephanie even has an outdoor bakery, which is perfect for garden parties—her favorite type of party. Here, Stephanie has just put the finishing touches to her party preparations. She has set up the outdoor table and umbrella and is waiting for her friends to arrive.

Stephanie carefully pours the cake ingredients into a large bowl. After thoroughly mixing, she pops it into her outdoor oven.

Stephanie loves to explore Heartlake City in her stylish purple and blue convertible. She loads her puppy Coco into the back and picks up her friends for the ride.

The girls drive to their favorite hangouts—the beach, the beauty shop, or the café. But Stephanie likes to plan more challenging adventures, too.

Grooming equipment

Windshield

MP3 player

Dog grooming basket

Stephanie fills up the bucket from the street faucet and adds car shampoo. She is ready to scrub!

The friends take road trips along the coast, to the forest, and even as far as the Clearspring Mountains at the edge of Heartlake City.

Stephanie is very proud of her car and likes to keep it clean and sparkling. She even manages to make washing her car fun! She listens to party tunes on her MP3 player and dances while she scrubs. Sometimes she washes Coco at the same time, too!

Secret hangout

Ssh! Don't tell anyone, but this is the secret headquarters of the Friends Club! Olivia found the treehouse on the day she moved to Heartlake City, and it is very close to her house. When she met Stephanie, Mia, Andrea, and Emma, she knew the treehouse would be the perfect hangout for the girls.

Practical Olivia and Emma both checked that the treehouse was safe, and all the friends worked together to create a beautiful girls-only space. They even fixed the cool folding ladder, which they lift up to stop anyone else from sneaking into their treehouse.

Bench

Lookout

Telescope

Folding ladder

Secret box

The girls like to camp out in their treehouse. Stephanie brings cupcakes for a midnight feast, and the friends share their secrets, hopes, and dreams under the beautiful night sky. The club telescope comes in handy to check that nobody is listening nearby!

Far and away
The girls can see Lake Heart, the ocean, and the Clearspring Mountains through the club telescope.

No secret club headquarters would be complete without a special hiding place. The girls keep their most treasured possessions inside a blue box. It is hidden at the base of the treehouse underneath tree branches. The friends love to search for treasure. One day, they hope to uncover Dark-Eyed Kate's pirate treasure on Lighthouse Island.

The treehouse can also be used as a temporary animal hospital. One day, Olivia and her friends found a poor yellow bird with a broken wing in their new treehouse headquarters. They named him Goldie and worked hard to nurse him back to health. The girls even built a red and white stripy birdhouse, which sits under the tree. Goldie liked his new home so much that he has stayed!

The girls worked together to build a bed for Maxie and a birdhouse for Goldie.

Olivia also found a stray cat, Maxie. She has become the club headquarters' resident cat. Andrea brings leftover fish and milk from the café as treats for Maxie. The little kitten likes to join the girls at their sleepovers, so they have made a cute little bed for Maxie to sleep in.

Friends forever

A lot has changed in Olivia's life over the past few months. She has moved to an amazing new town and made four wonderful best friends. Life is pretty great! Olivia, Emma, Andrea, Stephanie, and Mia have so much fun together and they always look out for each other. Olivia feels like she has known her four new friends forever, and can't wait to have many more adventures with them. She is sure that they will always be best friends.

Olivia's diary
Olivia has so much to write about! Her diary is packed with tales of her new friends and their adventures.

Quiz

1. Where does Olivia like to write her diary?

2. Which musical instrument does Andrea play?

3. What object does Emma take with her everywhere?

4. What is the name of Mia's horse?

5. What does Stephanie always do on her friends' birthdays?

1. On the swing, 2. Piano, 3. Her camera, 4. Bella, 5. Bake a cake